Hooked on Crochet!™
HATS™

General Information

Many of the products used in this pattern book can be purchased from local craft, fabric and variety stores, or from the Annie's Attic Needlecraft Catalog (see Customer Service information on page 31).

Contents

Easy Tam

DESIGN BY **KIMBERLY KOTARY**

SKILL LEVEL
■■■□
INTERMEDIATE

FINISHED SIZE
One size fits most adults

MATERIALS
- N. Y. Yarns Rocky bulky (chunky) weight yarn (1¾ oz/ 98 yds/50g per ball):
  2 balls each #004 brick mix and #005 cadet blue mix
- Size K/10½/6.5mm crochet hook or size needed to obtain gauge
- Stitch markers

5 BULKY

GAUGE
12 sc = 4 inches; 13 sc rnds = 4 inches

PATTERN NOTES
Work in continuous rounds; do not turn or join unless otherwise stated.

Mark first stitch of each round.

INSTRUCTIONS
TAM
Rnd 1: With blue, ch 2, 6 sc in 2nd ch from hook, **do not join** (see Pattern Notes). (6 sc)

Rnd 2: 2 sc in each st around. (12 sc)

Rnd 3: [2 sc in next st, sc in next st] around. (18 sc)

Rnd 4: [2 sc in next st, sc in each of next 2 sts] around. (24 sc)

Rnd 5: [2 sc in next st, sc in each of next 3 sts] around. (30 sc)

Rnd 6: [2 sc in next st, sc in each of next 4 sts] around. (36 sc)

Rnd 7: [2 sc in next st, sc in each of next 5 sts] around. (42 sc)

Rnd 8: [2 sc in next st, sc in each of next 6 sts] around. (48 sc)

Rnd 9: [2 sc in next st, sc in each of next 7 sts] around. (54 sc)

Rnd 10: [2 sc in next st, sc in each of next 8 sts] around. (60 sc)

Rnd 11: [2 sc in next st, sc in each of next 9 sts] around. (66 sc)

Rnd 12: [2 sc in next st, sc in each of next 10 sts] around. (72 sc)

Rnd 13: [2 sc in next st, sc in each of next 11 sts] around. (78 sc)

Rnd 14: [2 sc in next st, sc in each of next 12 sts] around. (84 sc)

Rnd 15: [2 sc in next st, sc in each of next 13 sts] around. (90 sc)

Rnd 16: [2 sc in next st, sc in each of next 14 sts] around. Fasten off. (96 sc)

Rnd 17: Working in **back lps** (see Stitch Guide), join brick with sc in first st, sc in each st around.

Rnd 18: [**Sc dec** (see Stitch Guide) in next 2 sts, sc in each of next 14 sts] (90 sc)

Rnd 19: [Sc dec in next 2 sts, sc in each of next 13 sts] around. (84 sc)

Rnd 20: [Sc dec in next 2 sts, sc in each of next 12 sts] around. (78 sc)

Rnd 21: [Sc dec in next 2 sts, sc in each of next 11 sts] around. (72 sc)

Rnd 22: [Sc dec in next 2 sts, sc in each of next 10 sts] around. *(66 sc)*

Rnd 23: [Sc dec in next 2 sts, sc in each of next 9 sts] around. *(60 sc)*

Rnd 24: [Sc dec in next 2 sts, sc in each of next 8 sts] around. *(54 sc)*

Rnd 25: [Sc dec in next 2 sts, sc in each of next 7 sts] around. *(48 sc)*

Rnd 26: [Sc dec in next 2 sts, sc in each of next 6 sts] around. *(42 sc)*

Rnd 27: Sl st in each st around. Fasten off. ■

BOHO Beanie

DESIGN BY **JEWDY LAMBERT**

SKILL LEVEL

INTERMEDIATE

FINISHED SIZE
One size fits most adults

MATERIALS
- Medium (worsted) weight wool yarn: 2 oz/100 yds/57g each brown and variegated green/brown
- Size I/9/5.5mm crochet hook or size needed to obtain gauge

GAUGE
3 dc = inch; 3 dc rows = 1¾ inches

PATTERN NOTES
Chain-2 at beginning of row or round counts as first double crochet unless otherwise stated.

Join with slip stitch as indicated unless otherwise stated.

Always change colors in last stitch.

Work over yarn carried behind work and pick up again when needed.

INSTRUCTIONS
BEANIE
Rnd 1: With brown, ch 4, sl st in first ch to form ring, **ch 2** *(see Pattern Notes)*, 15 dc in ring, **join** *(see Pattern Notes)* in 2nd ch of beg ch-2. *(16 dc)*

Rnd 2: Ch 2, dc in same st, 2 dc in each st around, join in 2nd ch of beg ch-2. *(32 dc)*

Rnd 3: Ch 2, dc in same st, 2 dc in each st around, join in 2nd ch of beg ch-2. *(64 dc)*

Rnd 4: Ch 2, dc in next st, **changing colors** *(see Stitch Guide and Pattern Notes)* to variegated in last st, *dc in each of next 2 sts changing to brown, dc in each of next 2 sts** changing to variegated, rep from * around, ending last rep at **, join in 2nd ch of beg ch-2.

Rnd 5: With brown, ch 2, dc in each st around, join in 2nd ch of beg ch-2.

Rnd 6: Ch 2, *changing to variegated, sc in each of next 3 sts, changing to brown**, sc in each of next 2 sts, rep from * around, ending last rep at **, join in 2nd ch of beg ch-2.

Rnd 7: With brown, ch 2, dc in each st around changing to variegated, join in 2nd ch of beg ch-2.

Rnd 8: Ch 2, dc in next st, changing to variegated in last st, [dc in each of next 2 sts changing to brown, dc in each of next 2 sts, changing to variegated] around, join in 2nd ch of beg ch-2.

Rnd 9: With variegated, ch 2, dc in each st around, join in 2nd ch of beg ch-2.

Rnd 10: Ch 2, *changing to brown, sc in each of next 3 sts, changing to variegated**, sc in each of next 2 sts, rep from * around, ending last rep at **, join in 2nd ch of beg ch-2.

Rnd 11: With variegated, ch 2, dc in each st around changing to brown, join in 2nd ch of beg ch-2.

Rnds 12 & 13: Ch 2, dc in each st around, join in 2nd ch of beg ch-2.

Rnd 14: Ch 2, dc in each st around to variegated, join in 2nd ch of beg ch-2.

Rnd 15: Ch 1, sc in each st around, join in beg sc. Fasten off both colors.

TOP
Join with **fpsl st** *(see Stitch Guide)* around any st on rnd 1, ch 10, [sk next st, fpsl st round next st, ch 10] around, fpsl st around next st changing to brown, [ch 15, sk next st, fpsl st around next st] around, ending with ch 15, join in beg sl st. Fasten off. ∎

Cranberry Cloche

DESIGN BY ANNA AL

SKILL LEVEL

INTERMEDIATE

FINISHED SIZE
One size fits most adults

MATERIALS
- Medium (worsted) weight cotton: 3½ oz/175 yds/100g red
- Size G/6/4mm crochet hook or size needed to obtain gauge

4 MEDIUM

GAUGE
4 hdc = 1 inch; 11 hdc rnds = 3 inches

PATTERN NOTES
Join with slip stitch as indicated unless otherwise stated.

Chain-2 at beginning of row or round does not count as first half double crochet unless otherwise stated.

Chain-3 at beginning of row or round counts as first double crochet unless otherwise stated.

INSTRUCTIONS
CLOCHE
Rnd 1: Ch 3, 8 hdc in 3rd ch from hook, **join** (see Pattern Notes) in beg hdc. (8 hdc)

Rnd 2: Ch 2 (see Pattern Notes), 2 hdc in first st and in each st around, join in beg hdc. (16 hdc)

Rnds 3: Ch 2, 2 hdc in first st, hdc in next st, [2 hdc in next st, hdc in next st] around, join in beg hdc. (24 hdc)

Rnd 4: Ch 2, 2 hdc in first st, hdc in each of next 2 sts, [2 hdc in next st, hdc in each of next 2 sts] around, join in beg hdc. (32 hdc)

Rnd 5: Ch 2, 2 hdc in first st, hdc in each of next 3 sts, [2 hdc in next st, hdc in each of next 3 sts] around, join in beg hdc. (40 hdc)

Rnd 6: Ch 2, 2 hdc in first st, hdc in each of next 4 sts, [2 hdc in next st, hdc in each of next 4 sts] around, join in beg hdc. (48 hdc)

Rnd 7: Ch 2, 2 hdc in first st, hdc in each of next 5 sts, [2 hdc in next st, hdc in each of next 5 sts] around, join in beg hdc. (56 hdc)

Rnd 8: Ch 2, 2 hdc in first st, hdc in each of next 6 sts, [2 hdc in next st, hdc in each of next 6 sts] around, join in beg hdc. (64 hdc)

Rnd 9: Ch 2, 2 hdc in first st, hdc in each of next 7 sts, [2 hdc in next st, hdc in each of next 7 sts] around, join in beg hdc. (72 hdc)

Rnd 10: Ch 2, 2 hdc in first st, hdc in each of next 8 sts, [2 hdc in next st, hdc in each of next 8 sts] around, join in beg hdc. (80 hdc)

Rnd 11: Ch 2, 2 hdc in first st, hdc in each of next 19 sts, [2 hdc in next st, hdc in each of next 19 sts] around, join in beg hdc. (84 hdc)

Rnd 12: Ch 1, sc in first st, *sk next 2 sts, 5 dc in next st, sk next 2 sts**, sc in next st, rep from * around, ending last rep at **, join in beg sc.

Rnd 13: Ch 3 (see Pattern Notes), 4 dc in same st, *sc in center dc of next dc group**, 5 dc in next sc, rep from * around, ending last rep at **, join in 3rd ch of beg ch-3.

Rnd 14: Sl st in next st, ch 1, sc in next st, *5 dc in next sc**, sc in center st of next dc group, rep from * around, ending last rep at **, join in beg sc.

Next rnds: [Rep rnds 13 and 14 alternately] until piece measures 4½ inches from rnd 12 or to desired length. At end of last rnd, fasten off. ■

Soft & Cozy Hat

DESIGN BY LAURA GEBHARDT

SKILL LEVEL

EASY

FINISHED SIZE
One size fits most adults

MATERIALS

- Patons Bohemian super bulky (super chunky) weight yarn (2¾ oz/68 yds/80g per ball):
  1 ball #11110 indigo indulgence
- Size N/15/10mm crochet hook or size needed to obtain gauge
- Tapestry needle
- Stitch marker

6 SUPER BULKY

GAUGE
9 sc = 4 inches; 4 rnds = 2 inches

PATTERN NOTES
Work in continuous rounds; do not turn or join unless otherwise stated.

Mark first stitch of each round.

INSTRUCTIONS

HAT

Rnd 1: Ch 2, 6 sc in 2nd ch from hook, **do not join** *(see Pattern Notes)*. *(6 sc)*

Rnd 2: 2 sc in each sc around. *(12 sc)*

Rnd 3: [Sc in next sc, 2 sc in next sc] around. *(18 sc)*

Rnd 4: Sc in each sc around.

Rnd 5: [Sc in each of next 2 sc, 2 sc in next sc] around. *(24 sc)*

Rnd 6: [Sc in each of next 3 sc, 2 sc in next sc] around. *(30 sc)*

Rnd 7: Sc in each sc around.

Rnd 8: [Sc in each of next 2 sc, 2 sc in next sc] around. *(40 sc)*

Rnds 9 & 10: Sc in each sc around.

Rnd 11: [Sc in each of next 4 sc, 2 sc in next sc] around. *(48 sc)*

Rnds 12–14: Sc in each sc around.

Rnd 15: Ch 3 *(counts as first dc)*, 2 dc in next sc, [dc in next sc, 2 dc in next sc] around, join with sl st in 3rd ch of beg ch-3. Fasten off. *(72 dc)* ■

Warm & Fuzzy
Toque Hat

DESIGN BY KATHERINE ENG

SKILL LEVEL

INTERMEDIATE

FINISHED SIZE
One size fits most adults

MATERIALS
- N. Y. Yarns Cloud bulky (chunky) weight yarn (1¾ oz/105 yds/50g per skein): 1 skein #1 lightning
- N. Y. Yarns La La bulky (chunky) weight yarn (1¾ oz/92 yds/50g per skein): 1 skein #1 white
- Sizes I/9/5.5mm and P/15/10mm crochet hooks or size needed to obtain gauge

GAUGE
Size P hook: Rnds 1 & 2 = 2½ inches in diameter

PATTERN NOTE
Join with slip stitch as indicated unless otherwise stated.

INSTRUCTIONS
TOQUE
Rnd 1: With size P hook and lightning, ch 4, sl st in first ch to form ring, ch 1, 8 sc in ring, **join** (*see Pattern Note*) in beg sc. (*8 sc*)

Rnd 2: Ch 1, 2 sc in each st around, join in beg sc. (*16 sc*)

Rnd 3: Ch 1, 2 sc in first st, sc in next st, [2 sc in next st, sc in next st] around, join in beg sc. (*24 sc*)

Rnd 4: Ch 1, 2 sc in first st, sc in each of next 2 sts, [2 sc in next st, sc in each of next 2 sts] around, join in beg sc. (*32 sc*)

Rnd 5: Ch 1, 2 sc in first st, sc in each of next 3 sts, [2 sc in next st, sc in each of next 3 sts] around, join in beg sc. (*40 sc*)

Rnds 6–8: Ch 1, sc in each st around, join in beg sc.

Rnd 9: Ch 1, sc in each of first 2 sts, [ch 2, sk next 2 sts, sc in each of next 2 sts] around, ch 2, sk last 2 sts, join in beg sc.

Rnds 10–14: Ch 1, sc in each of first 2 sts, [ch 2, sk next ch sp, sc in each of next 2 sts] around, ending with ch 2, sk last ch sp, join in beg sc.

Rnd 15: Ch 1, sc in each st around with 2 sc in each ch sp, join in beg sc. Fasten off.

Rnd 16: With size I hook, join white with sc in first st, sc in each st around, join in beg sc.

Rnd 17: Ch 1, [sl st in next st, ch 1] around, join in joining sl st of last rnd. Fasten off.

TOP LOOP
With size I hook and 2 strands white held tog, leaving 2-inch end at beg, ch 12, sl st in first ch to form ring. Leaving 2-inch end, fasten off.

Using 2-inch ends, attach Top Loop to center of rnd 1. ■

Striped
BEANIE

DESIGN BY DONNA CHILDS

SKILL LEVEL

INTERMEDIATE

FINISHED SIZE
One size fits most adults

MATERIALS
- DK (light worsted) weight yarn: 1¾ oz/154 yds/50g each black and citrine
- Size F/5/3.75mm crochet hook or size needed to obtain gauge

GAUGE
18 dc = 4 inches; 10 dc rnds = 4 inches

PATTERN NOTES
Chain-3 at beginning of row or round counts as first double crochet unless otherwise stated.

Join with slip stitch as indicated unless otherwise stated.

INSTRUCTIONS
HAT
Rnd 1: With citrine, ch 4, sl st in first ch to form ring, **ch 3** (see Pattern Notes), 11 dc in ring, **join** (see Pattern Notes) in 3rd ch of beg ch-3. (12 dc)

Rnd 2: Ch 3, 2 dc in each st around, dc in same st as beg ch-3, join in 3rd ch of beg ch-3. (24 dc)

Rnd 3: Ch 3, dc in next st, [2 dc in next st, dc in next st] around, dc in same st as beg ch-3, join in 3rd ch of beg ch-3. (36 dc)

Rnd 4: Ch 3, dc in each of next 2 sts, [2 dc in next st, dc in each of next 2 sts] around, dc in same st as beg ch-3, join in 3rd ch of beg ch-3. (48 dc)

Rnd 5: Ch 3, dc in each of next 3 sts, [2 dc in next st, dc in each of next 3 sts] around, dc in same st as beg ch-3, join in 3rd ch of beg ch-3. (60 dc)

Rnd 6: Ch 3, dc in each of next 4 sts, [2 dc in next st, dc in each of next 4 sts] around, dc in same st as beg ch-3, join in 3rd ch of beg ch-3. (72 dc)

Rnd 7: Ch 3, dc in each of next 5 sts, [2 dc in next st, dc in each of next 5 sts] around, dc in same st as beg ch-3, join in 3rd ch of beg ch-3. (84 dc)

Rnd 8: Ch 3, dc in each st around, join in 3rd ch of beg ch-3.

Rnd 9: Ch 3, dc in each of next 6 sts, [2 dc in next st, dc in each of next 6 sts] around, dc in same st as beg ch-3, join in 3rd ch of beg ch-3. (96 dc)

Rnds 10–12: Ch 3, dc in each st around, join in 3rd ch of beg ch-3. At end of last rnd, fasten off.

Rnd 13: Join black in first st, ch 3, dc in each st around, join in 3rd ch of beg ch-3.

Rnd 14: Ch 3, dc in each st around, join in 3rd ch of beg ch-3. Fasten off.

Rnd 15: Join citrine in first st, ch 3, dc in each st around, join in 3rd ch of beg ch-3. Fasten off.

Rnd 16: Join black in first st, ch 3, dc in each st around, join in 3rd ch of beg ch-3.

Rnd 17: Ch 3, dc in each st around, join in 3rd ch of beg ch-3. Fasten off.

Rnd 18: Join citrine in first st, ch 3, dc in each st around, join in 3rd ch of beg ch-3.

Rnds 19 & 20: Ch 3, dc in each st around, join in 3rd ch of beg ch-3. At end of last rnd, fasten off. ■

Summertime
Hat
DESIGN BY MICKIE AKINS

SKILL LEVEL
■■□□
EASY

FINISHED SIZE
One size fits most adults

MATERIALS

- Red Heart LusterSheen fine (sport) weight yarn (4 oz/335 yds/113g per skein):
  2 skeins #0235 think pink
- Size G/6/4mm crochet hook or size needed to obtain gauge

GAUGE
With 2 strands held tog: 4 sc = 1 inch; 4 sc rnds = 1 inch

PATTERN NOTES
Use 2 strands of yarn held together unless otherwise stated.

Join with slip stitch as indicated unless otherwise stated.

INSTRUCTIONS
HAT
Rnd 1: With 2 strands held tog (*see Pattern Notes*), ch 2, 6 sc in 2nd ch from hook, **join** (*see Pattern Notes*) in beg sc. (*6 sc*)

Rnd 2: Ch 1, 2 sc in each st around, join in beg sc. (*12 sc*)

Rnd 3: Ch 1, sc in first st, 2 sc in next st, [sc in next st, 2 sc in next st] around, join in beg sc. (*18 sc*)

Rnd 4: Ch 1, sc in each of first 2 sts, 2 sc in next st, [sc in each of next 2 sts, 2 sc in next st] around, join in beg sc. (*24 sc*)

Rnd 5: Ch 1, sc in each of first 3 sts, 2 sc in next st, [sc in each of next 3 sts, 2 sc in next st] around, join in beg sc. (*30 sc*)

Rnd 6: Ch 1, sc in each of first 4 sts, 2 sc in next st, [sc in each of next 4 sts, 2 sc in next st] around, join in beg sc. (*36 sc*)

Rnd 7: Ch 1, sc in each of first 5 sts, 2 sc in next st, [sc in each of next 5 sts, 2 sc in next st] around, join in beg sc. (*42 sc*)

Rnd 8: Ch 1, sc in each of first 3 sts, [2 sc in next st, sc in each of next 6 sts] around to last 4 sts, 2 sc in next st, sc in each of last 3 sts, join in beg sc. (*48 sc*)

Rnd 9: Ch 1, 2 sc in first st, sc in each of next 7 sts, [2 sc in next st, sc in each of next 7 sts] around, join in beg sc. (*54 sc*)

Rnd 10: Ch 1, sc in each of first 4 sts, [2 sc in next st, sc in each of next 8 sts] around to last 5 sts, 2 sc in next st, sc in each of last 4 sts, join in beg sc. (*60 sc*)

Rnd 11: Ch 1, sc in each of first 9 sts, 2 sc in next st, [sc in each of next 9 sts, 2 sc in next st] around, join in beg sc. (*66 sc*)

Rnd 12: Ch 1, 2 sc in first st, sc in each of next 10 sts, [2 sc in next st, sc in each of next 10 sts] around, join in beg sc. (*72 sc*)

Rnd 13: Ch 1, sc in each of first 6 sts, [2 sc in next st, sc in each of next 11 sts] around to last 6 sts, 2 sc in next st, sc in each of last 5 sts, join in beg sc. (*78 sc*)

Rnd 14: Ch 1, 2 sc in first st, sc in each of next 12 sts, [2 sc in next st, sc in each of next 12 sts] around, join in beg sc. (*84 sc*)

Rnd 15: Ch 1, sc in each of first 7 sts, [2 sc in next st, sc in each of next 13 sts] around to last 7 sts, 2 sc in next st, sc in each of last 6 sts, join in beg sc. *(90 sc)*

Rnds 16–31: Ch 1, sc in each st around, join in beg sc.

Rnd 32: Working in **front lps** *(see Stitch Guide)*, ch 1, 2 sc in first st, sc in each of next 4 sts, [2 sc in next st, sc in each of next 4 sts] around, join in beg sc. *(108 sc)*

Rnds 33–36: Working in both lps, ch 1, sc in each st around, join in beg sc.

Rnd 37: Ch 1, 2 sc in first st, sc in each of next 5 sts, [2 sc in next st, sc in each of next 5 sts] around, join in beg sc. *(126 sc)*

Rnds 38–42: Ch 1, sc in each st around, join in beg sc.

Rnd 43: Ch 1, sl st in each st around, join in beg sl st. Fasten off. ∎

Teen Earflap Hat

DESIGN BY SHEILA LESLIE

SKILL LEVEL
■■□□
EXPERIENCED

FINISHED SIZE
One size fits most teens

MATERIALS
- Red Heart Super Saver medium (worsted) weight yarn (7 oz/364 yds/198g per skein): 1 skein each #378 claret, #320 cornmeal, #336 warm brown, #311 white and #321 gold

- Size H/8/5mm crochet hook or size needed to obtain gauge
- Stitch markers

GAUGE
7 sc = 2 inches; 9 sc rnds = 2 inches

PATTERN NOTES
Work in continuous rounds, do not turn or join unless otherwise stated.

Join with slip stitch as indicated unless otherwise stated.

Mark first stitch of each round.

Always change colors in last stitch.

Work over yarn carried behind work and pick up again when needed.

SPECIAL STITCHES
Long single crochet (lng sc): Insert hook in place indicated, pull up long lp even with this row and complete sc.

Cluster (cl): Holding back last lp of each st on hook, 4 dc in place indicated, yo, pull through all lps on hook.

INSTRUCTIONS
HAT
Rnd 1: With claret, ch 2, 6 sc in 2nd ch from hook, **do not join** (see Pattern Notes). (6 sc)

Rnd 2: 2 sc in each st around. (12 sc)

Rnd 3: [Sc in next st, 2 sc in next st] around. (18 sc)

Rnd 4: [Sc in each of next 2 sts, 2 sc in next st] around. (24 sc)

Rnd 5: [2 sc in next st, sc in each of next 3 sts] around. (30 sc)

Rnd 6: [Sc in each of next 4 sts, 2 sc in next st] around. (36 sc)

Rnd 7: [Sc in each of next 5 sts, 2 sc in next st] around, **join** (see Pattern Notes) in beg sc. Fasten off. (42 sc)

Rnd 8: Join cornmeal with sc in first st, sc in same st, sc in each of next 6 sts, [2 sc in next st, sc in each of next 6 sts] around. (48 sc)

Rnd 9: [Sc in each of next 7 sts, 2 sc in next st] around. (54 sc)

Rnd 10: [Sc in each of next 8 sts, 2 sc in next st] around. *(60 sc)*

Rnd 11: Sc in each st around, join in beg sc. Fasten off.

Rnd 12: Join warm brown with sc in first st, **lng sc** *(see Special Stitches)* in st 1 rnd below, sc in next st on this rnd, lng sc in next st 2 rnds below, 2 sc in next st on this rnd, *[lng sc in next st 1 rnd below, sc in next st on this rnd, lng sc in next st 2 rnds below, sc in next st on this rnd] twice, lng sc in next st 1 rnd below, 2 sc in next st**, [lng sc in next st 2 rnds below, sc in next st on this rnd, lng sc in next st 1 rnd below, sc in next st on this rnd] twice, lng sc in next st 2 rnds below, 2 sc in next st, rep from * around, ending last rep at **, lng sc in next st 2 rnds below, sc in next st on this rnd, lng sc in next st 1 rnd below, sc in next st on this rnd, lng sc in next st 2 rnds below, join in beg sc. *(66 sts)*

Rnd 13: Ch 1, sc in first st, sc in next st, **changing colors** *(see Stitch Guide and Pattern Notes)* to white in last st, sc in next st, changing to brown, [sc in each of next 2 sts, changing to white, sc in next st, changing to brown] around, join in beg sc. Fasten off white.

Rnd 14: Ch 1, sc in each of first 10 sts, 2 sc in next st, [sc in each of next 10 sts, 2 sc in next st] around, join in beg sc. Fasten off. *(72 sc)*

Rnd 15: Join claret with sc in first st, sc in each st around, join in beg sc. Fasten off.

Rnd 16: Join gold with sc in first st, sc in each st around, join in beg sc. Fasten off.

Rnd 17: Join white with sc in first st, sc in each st around, join in beg sc.

Rnds 18 & 19: Ch 1, sc in each st around, join with sl st in beg sc. At end of last rnd, fasten off.

Rnd 20: Join gold with sc in first st, *sc in each of next 2 sts, lng sc in next st on rnd 16**, sc in next st on this rnd, rep from * around, ending last rep at **, join in beg sc.

Rnd 21: Ch 1, sc in each st around, join in beg sc. Fasten off.

Rnd 22: Join claret with sc in first st, sc in each st around, join in beg sc.

Rnd 23: Ch 1, sc in each st around, join in beg sc.

Rnd 24: Ch 1, sc in each of first 3 sts, changing to white, *sc in next st, changing to claret**, sc in each of next 3 sts, changing to white, rep from * around, ending last rep at **, join in beg sc. Fasten off white.

Rnds 25 & 26: Ch 1, sc in each st around, join in beg sc. At end of last rnd, **turn.** Fasten off.

Rnd 27: With WS facing, join white with sc in last sc before joining, sc in each of next 2 sts, *cl *(see Special Stitches)* in next st**, sc in each of next 3 sts, rep from * around, ending last rep at **, join in beg sc, turn. Fasten off.

Rnd 28: With RS facing, join brown with sc in st before joining, sc in each of next 3 sts *changing to cornmeal, sc in each of next 4 sts, changing to brown**, sc in each of next 4 sts, rep from * around, ending last rep at **, join in beg sc.

Rnd 29: Ch 1, sc in each of first 4 sts, changing to cornmeal, [sc in each of next 4 sts, changing to brown, sc in each of next 4 sts, changing to cornmeal] around, join in beg sc.

Rnds 30 & 31: Ch 1, sc in each of first 4 sts, changing to brown, *sc in each of next 4 sts, changing to cornmeal**, sc in each of next 4 sts, changing to brown, rep from * around, ending last rep at **, join in beg sc. Fasten off.

FIRST EAR FLAP
Row 1: Now working in rows, sk first 11 sts, join claret with sc in next st, sc in each of next 12 sts, leaving rem sts unworked, turn. *(13 sc)*

Rows 2 & 3: Ch 1, sc in each st across, turn.

Row 4: Ch 1, **sc dec** *(see Stitch Guide)* in first 2 sts, sc in each st across with sc dec in last 2 sts, turn. Fasten off. *(11 sc)*

Row 5: Join cornmeal with sc in first st, sc in each st across, turn.

Row 6: Ch 1, sc dec in first 2 sts, sc in st across with sc dec in last 2 sts, turn. *(9 sc)*

Row 7: Ch 1, sc in each st across, turn.

Row 8: Ch 1, sc in each st across, turn. Fasten off.

Row 9: Join claret with sl st in first st, sc dec in same st and next st, sc in each st across with sc dec in last 2 sts, turn. *(7 sc)*

Row 10: Ch 1, sc in each st across, turn.

Row 11: Ch 1, sc dec in first 2 sts, sc in each st across with sc dec in last 2 sts, turn. *(5 sc)*

Row 12: Ch 1, sc dec in first 2 sts, sc in next st, sc dec in last 2 sts. Fasten off. *(3 sc)*

2ND EAR FLAP

Row 1: Sk first 26 sts from First Ear Flap, join claret with sc in next st, sc in each of next 12 sts, leaving rem sts unworked, turn. *(13 sc)*

Rows 2–12: Rep rows 2–12 of First Ear Flap.

EDGING

Join claret with sc in 2nd st after sl st at center back, sc in each of next 9 sts, *sc in same st as first st of Ear Flap, evenly sp 12 sc across in end of rows, 2 sc in first st, sc in next st, 2 sc in next st, evenly sp 12 sc across in end of rows, sc in same st as last sc of row of Ear Flap*, sc in each of next 26 sts, rep between * once, sc in each st across, join in beg sc. Fasten off.

TIE
MAKE 2.

Cut 9 strands of claret, each 36 inches in length. Tie separate strand around center of all strands.

Divide strands into 3 sections and braid until about 11 inches long. Tie strand of claret at bottom of braid. Trim ends.

Attach 1 Tie to center bottom of last row on each Ear Flap.

TOP BRAID
MAKE 2.

Cut 9 strands of claret, each 21 inches in length. Tie separate strand around center of all strands.

Divide strands into 3 sections and braid until about 5 inches long. Tie strand of claret at bottom of braid. Trim ends.

Attach Top Braids to center top of Hat. ■

Autumn to Winter Hat

DESIGN BY KATHERINE ENG

SKILL LEVEL

INTERMEDIATE

FINISHED SIZE
One size fits most adults

MATERIALS
- N. Y. Yarns Tweed bulky (chunky) weight yarn (1¾ oz/76 yds/50g per ball):
  2 balls #2 autumn gold
- Size I/9/5.5mm crochet hook or size needed to obtain gauge
- Tapestry needle
- Decorative wood beads with large holes: 2

GAUGE
Rows 1–3 = 1½ x 6 inches

PATTERN NOTES
To make smaller hat, use smaller size hook.

Join rounds with slip stitch as indicated unless otherwise stated.

INSTRUCTIONS
HAT
Row 1: Ch 18, sc in 2nd ch from hook and in each ch across, turn. (*17 sc*)

Row 2: Ch 1, sc in **back lp** (*see Stitch Guide*) of each of first 5 sts, sc in **front lp** (*see Stitch Guide*) in each of next 12 sts (*top edge*), turn.

Row 3: Ch 1, sc in front lp of each of first 12 sts, sc in back lp of each of last 5 sts, turn.

Rows 4–50: [Rep rows 2 and 3 alternately] 24 times, ending last rep with row 2. At end of last row, leaving long end, fasten off.

Working in back lps, sew row 1 and row 50 tog, forming tube.

TOP
Rnd 1: Now working in rnds with seam at back, join with sc in end of first row at top edge, sc in end of each row around, **join** (*see Pattern Notes*) in beg sc. (*50 sc*)

Rnd 2: Working in front lps, ch 1, sc in each st around, join in beg sc.

Rnd 3: Ch 1, sc in first st, ch 1, sk next st, [sc in next st, ch 1, sk next st] around, join in beg sc.

Rnd 4: Sl st in first ch sp, ch 1, sc in same ch sp, sk all sts, sc in each ch sp around, join in beg sc. (*25 sc*)

Rnd 5: Ch 4 (*counts as first dc and ch-1*), [dc in next st, ch 1, sk next st] around, join in 3rd ch of beg ch-4.

Rnd 6: Sl st in next ch sp, ch 8, sl st in same ch sp, (sl st, ch 8, sl st) in each ch sp around, join in beg sl st. Fasten off.

TIE
Leaving 6-inch end, ch 70. Leaving 6-inch end, fasten off.

Weave ch under and over sts of rnd 5, beg and ending in back.

Pull to tighten and close center top. Tie in bow.

Thread 1 bead onto each end. Tie knot in each end to secure bead. Separate strands. Trim. ∎

Winter Toque

DESIGN BY MINETTE COLLINS SMITH

SKILL LEVEL

INTERMEDIATE

FINISHED SIZE

One size fits most adults

MATERIALS

- Medium (worsted) weight yarn: 2½ oz/125 yds/71g each variegated red and red cotton nubby
- Size H/8/5mm double-ended hook or size needed to obtain gauge
- Tapestry needle

4 MEDIUM

GAUGE

5 sts = 2 inches; 4 rows = 1 inch

SPECIAL STITCHES

Pull up loop (pull up lp): Insert hook in vertical bar (*see Fig. 1*), yo, pull lp through, leaving lp on hook.

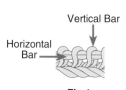

Vertical Bar

Horizontal Bar

Fig 1.
Vertical Bar

Work loops off hook (work lps off hook): Yo, pull through 1 lp on hook, [yo, pull through 2 lps on hook] across, leaving last st at end of row on hook. This is first vertical bar of next row.

Turn: Rotate hook 180 degrees and slide all lps to opposite end of hook. Do not turn unless otherwise stated.

Work loops off hook when adding a new color (work lps off hook when adding a new color): With new color, place slip knot on hook, pull slip knot through 1 lp on hook, [yo, pull through 2 lps on hook] across. Last lp rem on hook at end of row is first vertical bar of next row.

Work loops off hook with a color already in use (work lps off hook with a color already in use): Pick up color from row below, yo, pull through 1 lp on hook, [yo, pull through 2 lps on hook] across.

End a color that is no longer needed: Work across the row as stated and cut yarn, leaving a long end. Secure the end temporarily by tying to an adjacent yarn end, or permanently by weaving back through an inch or so on the row before.

Slip stitch in a vertical bar (sl st in a vertical bar): Insert hook under specified vertical bar, yo, pull through bar and lp on hook.

INSTRUCTIONS
HAT

Row 1: Using Special Stitches as needed, with cotton yarn, ch 32, **pull up lp** in 2nd ch from hook, pull up lp in each ch across, **turn**. (*32 sts*)

Row 2: With variegated yarn, **work lps off hook, do not turn.**

Row 3: Ch 1, sk first vertical bar, pull up lp in each vertical bar across, turn.

Row 4: With cotton yarn, work lps off hook, **do not turn.**

Row 5: Ch 1, sk first vertical bar, pull up lp in each vertical bar across, turn.

Rows 6–87: [Rep rows 2–5 consecutively] 21 times, ending last rep with row 3.

Row 88: Ch 1, **sl st in each vertical bar** across. Fasten off.

Matching sts, sew first and last rows tog.

TOP

Weave variegated yarn through ends of rows; pull tight to gather. Secure.

Fold ends of rows up on other side for cuff. ■

Bobble Beret

DESIGN BY SHEILA LESLIE

SKILL LEVEL

INTERMEDIATE

FINISHED SIZE
One size fits most adults

MATERIALS

- Red Heart Super Saver medium (worsted) weight yarn (7 oz/ 364 yds/198g per skein):
    1 skein #657 dusty teal
- Size J/10/6mm crochet hook or size needed to obtain gauge

GAUGE
7 hdc = 2 inches

PATTERN NOTES
Join with slip stitch as indicated unless otherwise stated.

Chain-2 at beginning of row or round counts as first half double crochet unless otherwise stated.

SPECIAL STITCH
Cluster (cl): Holding back last lp of each st on hook, 3 dc in place indicated, yo, pull through all lps on hook.

INSTRUCTIONS
BERET

Rnd 1: Ch 4, sl st in first ch to form ring, **ch 2** *(see Pattern Notes)*, 11 hdc in ring, **join** *(see Pattern Notes)* in 2nd ch of beg ch-2. *(12 hdc)*

Rnd 2: Ch 2, hdc in same st, 2 hdc in each st around, join in 2nd ch of beg ch-2. *(24 hdc)*

Rnd 3: Ch 2, 2 hdc in next st, [hdc in next st, 2 hdc in next st] around, join in 2nd ch of beg ch-2. *(36 hdc)*

Rnd 4: Ch 2, hdc in next st, 2 hdc in next st, [hdc in each of next 2 sts, 2 hdc in next st] around, join in 2nd ch of beg ch-2, **turn**. *(48 hdc)*

Rnd 5: Ch 1, **cl** *(see Special Stitch)* in first st, sc in next st, [cl in next st, sc in next st] around, join in top of first cl, turn.

Rnd 6: Ch 2, hdc in same st, hdc in each of next 3 sts, [2 hdc in next st, hdc in each of next 3 sts] around, join in 2nd ch of beg ch-2. *(60 hdc)*

Rnd 7: Ch 2, hdc in each st around, join in 2nd ch of beg ch-2.

Rnd 8: Ch 2, hdc in each of next 3 sts, 2 hdc in next st, [hdc in each of next 4 sts, 2 hdc in next st] around, join in 2nd ch of beg ch-2, turn. *(72 hdc)*

Rnd 9: Rep rnd 5.

Rnd 10: Ch 2, hdc in each of next 4 sts, 2 hdc in next st, [hdc in each of next 5 sts, 2 hdc in next st] around, join in 2nd ch of beg ch-2, turn. *(84 hdc)*

Rnd 11: Ch 2, hdc in each st around, join in 2nd ch of beg ch-2.

Rnd 12: Ch 2, hdc in each of next 5 sts, 2 hdc in next st, [hdc in each of next 6 sts, 2 hdc in next st] around, join in 2nd ch of beg ch-2, turn. *(96 hdc)*

Rnd 13: Rep rnd 5.

Rnd 14: Ch 2, hdc in each of next 6 sts, 2 hdc in next st, [hdc in each of next 7 sts, 2 hdc in next st] around, join in 2nd ch of beg ch-2. *(108 hdc)*

Rnd 15: Ch 2, hdc in each of next 7 sts, 2 hdc in next st, [hdc in each of next 8 sts, 2 hdc in next st] around, join in 2nd ch of beg ch-2. *(120 hdc)*

Rnd 16: Ch 2, hdc in each of next 8 sts, 2 hdc in next st, [hdc in each of next 9 sts, 2 hdc in next st] around, join in 2nd ch of beg ch-2, turn. *(132 hdc)*

Rnd 17: Rep rnd 5.

Rnds 18–20: Ch 2, hdc in each st around, join in 2nd ch of beg ch-2. At end of last row, turn.

Rnd 21: Ch 2, cl in first st, **sc dec** *(see Stitch Guide)* in next 2 sts, [cl in next st, sc dec in next 2 sts] around, join in 2nd ch of beg ch-2, turn. *(88 sts)*

Rnd 22: Ch 2, hdc in next st, **hdc dec** *(see Stitch Guide)* in next 2 sts, [hdc in each of next 2 sts, hdc dec in next 2 sts] around, join in 2nd ch of beg ch-2, turn. *(66 hdc)*

Rnd 23: Ch 1, sc in each of first 2 sts, sc dec in next 2 sts, [sc in each of next 2 sts, sc dec in next 2 sts] around, ending with sc in each of last 2 sts, join in beg sc. *(50 sc)*

Rnd 24: Ch 1, sc in each of first 23 sts, sc dec in next 2 sts, sc in each of next 23 sts, sc dec in last 2 sts, join in beg sc. *(48 sc)*

Rnds 25–27: Ch 1, sc in each st around, join in beg sc.

Rnd 28: Ch 1, sl st in each st around, join in beg sl st. Fasten off.

TOP TRIM
Leaving 12-inch end, ch 13, sc in 2nd ch from hook, cl in next ch, [sc in next ch, cl in next ch] around, join in beg sc. Fasten off.

Weave end through beg ch, pull closed. Sew to top of Beret. ■

Spring Fling Cloche

DESIGN BY KATHERINE ENG

SKILL LEVEL

■■■□
INTERMEDIATE

FINISHED SIZE
One size fits most adults

MATERIALS

- N. Y. Yarns Twinkle bulky (chunky) weight yarn (1¾ oz/ 92 yds/50g per ball):
  1 ball each #49 pinks and #21 sparkles
- Sizes I/9/5.5mm and P/15/10mm crochet hooks or size needed to obtain gauge
- Tapestry needle
- 12mm pink crystal bead: 1

GAUGE
Size P hook: Rnds 1 & 2 = 3¾ inches in diameter

PATTERN NOTES
Hold 1 strand of each color together unless otherwise stated.

Join with slip stitch as indicated unless otherwise stated.

Chain-4 at beginning of row or round counts as first double crochet and chain-1 unless otherwise stated.

Chain-3 at beginning of row or round counts as first double crochet unless otherwise stated.

SPECIAL STITCH
V-Stitch (V-st): (Dc, ch 1, dc) in place indicated.

INSTRUCTIONS
CLOCHE
Rnd 1: With 1 strand of each color held tog (*see Pattern Notes*) and size P hook, ch 4, sl st in first ch to form ring, ch 1, 8 sc in ring, **join** (*see Pattern Notes*) in beg sc. (*8 sc*)

Rnd 2: Ch 4 (*see Pattern Notes*), dc in same st, **V-st** (*see Special Stitch*) in each st around, join in 3rd ch of beg ch-4.

Rnd 3: Ch 4, sk next ch sp, dc in next st, ch 1, [dc in next st, ch 1, sk next ch sp, dc in next st, ch 1] around, join in 3rd ch of beg ch-4.

Rnd 4: Ch 3 (*see Pattern Notes*), dc in same st, ch 1, [2 dc in next st, ch 1] around, join in 3rd ch of beg ch-3.

Rnd 5: Ch 3, dc in same st, ch 2, sk next ch sp, [dc in each of next 2 sts, ch 2, sk next ch sp] around, join in 3rd ch of beg ch-3.

Rnd 6: Ch 3, dc in next st, ch 2, sk next ch sp, [dc in each of next 2 sts, ch 2, sk next ch sp] around, join in 3rd ch of beg ch-3.

Rnd 7: Ch 3, dc in next st, ch 1, sk next ch sp, [dc in each of next 2 sts, ch 1, sk next ch sp] around, join with sl st in 3rd ch of beg ch-3.

Rnd 8: Ch 1, sc in first st, sc in each st and in each ch sp around, join in beg sc.

HEADBAND
Row 1: Now working in rows, with size I hook, ch 5, sc in 2nd ch from hook and in each ch across, sl st in each of next 2 sts on Cloche, turn.

Row 2: Working in **back lps** (*see Stitch Guide*), sk sl sts, ch 1, sc in each of last 4 sts, turn.

Row 3: Working in back lps, ch 1, sc in each st across, sl st in each of next 2 sts on Cloche, turn.

Next rows: [Rep rows 2 and 3 alternately] around. At end of last row, leaving 5-inch end, fasten off.

Using end, sew last row and row 1 of Headband tog.

FLOWER

Rnd 1: With size I hook, ch 4, sl st in first ch to form ring, ch 1, 8 sc in ring, join. *(8 sc)*

Rnd 2: Ch 1, (sc, ch 4, sc) in first st, ch 3, [(sc, ch 4, sc) in next st, ch 3] around, join in beg sc. Fasten off.

Sew Flower to Cloche at seam. Sew bead to center of Flower. ■

Spring Fling Hat

DESIGN BY
JENNY KING

SKILL LEVEL

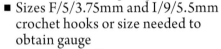

INTERMEDIATE

FINISHED SIZE
One size fits most adults

MATERIALS
- Cascade Fixation light (light worsted) weight elastic yarn (1¾ oz/ 100 yds/50g per ball): 1 ball #7360 taupe

  3 LIGHT

- Medium (worsted) weight suede yarn: 1 oz/50 yds/28g beige

  4 MEDIUM

- Sizes F/5/3.75mm and I/9/5.5mm crochet hooks or size needed to obtain gauge
- Tapestry needle
- Clear plastic canvas: 3 x 8 inch piece
- Large snap: 1

GAUGE
Size F hook and elastic yarn: 5 sts = 1 inch; 4 dc back lp rows = 1¼ inches

Size I hook and 1 strand each suede and elastic yarn held tog: 9 sts = 2 inches; 11 sc back lp rows = 3 inches

PATTERN NOTE
Join with slip stitch as indicated unless otherwise stated.

INSTRUCTIONS
HAT
Rnd 1: Starting at crown, with size I hook and 1 strand each suede and elastic yarn held tog, ch 11, 5 sc in 2nd ch from hook, sc in each of next 5 chs, hdc in each of next 3 chs (*front side of Hat*), 5 dc in last ch, working on opposite side of ch, hdc in each of next 3 chs, sc in each of last 5 chs (*back side of Hat*), **join** (*see Pattern Note*) in beg sc. (*26 sts*)

Rnd 2: Work rnds 2–12 in **back lps** (*see Stitch Guide*), ch 1, 2 sc in each of first 5 sts, sc in each of next 5 sts, hdc in each of next 3 sts, 2 dc in each of next 5 sts, hdc in each of next 3 sts, sc in each of last 5 sts, join in beg sc. (*36 sc*)

Rnd 3: Ch 1, 2 sc in first st, *[sc in next st, 2 sc in next st] 4 times, sc in each of next 9 sts*, 2 sc in next st, rep between * once, join in beg sc. (*46 sc*)

Rnd 4: Ch 1, 2 sc in first st, *[sc in each of next 2 sts, 2 sc in next st] 4 times, sc in each of next 10 sts*, 2 sc in next st, rep between * once, join in beg sc. (*56 sc*)

Rnd 5: Ch 1, 2 sc in first st, *[sc in each of next 3 sts, 2 sc in next st] 4 times, sc in each of next 11 sts*, 2 sc in next st, rep between * once, join in beg sc. *(66 sc)*

Rnd 6: Ch 1, 2 sc in first st, *[sc in each of next 4 sts, 2 sc in next st] 4 times, sc in each of next 12 sts*, 2 sc in next st, rep between * once, join in beg sc. *(76 sc)*

Rnd 7: Ch 1, 2 sc in first st, *[sc in each of next 5 sts, 2 sc in next st] 4 times, sc in each of next 13 sts*, 2 sc in next st, rep between * once, join in beg sc. *(86 sc)*

Rnd 8: Ch 1, 2 sc in first st, *[sc in each of next 6 sts, 2 sc in next st] 4 times, sc in each of next 14 sts*, 2 sc in next st, rep between * once, join in beg sc. *(96 sc)*

Rnd 9: Ch 1, 2 sc in first st, *[sc in each of next 7 sts, 2 sc in next st] 4 times, sc in each of next 15 sts*, 2 sc in next st, rep between * once, join in beg sc. *(106 sc)*

Rnd 10: Ch 1, 2 sc in first st, *[sc in each of next 8 sts, 2 sc in next st] 4 times, sc in each of next 16 sts*, 2 sc in next st, rep between * once, join in beg sc. *(116 sc)*

Rnd 11: Ch 1, 2 sc in first st, *[sc in each of next 9 sts, 2 sc in next st] 4 times, sc in each of next 17 sts*, 2 sc in next st, rep between * once, join in beg sc. *(126 sc)*

Rnd 12: Ch 1, sc in each of first 45 sts, dc in each of next 18 sts, sc in each of next 45 sts, dc in each of last 18 sts, join in beg sc, **turn**. Fasten off suede yarn only.

Rnd 13: With size F hook and elastic yarn, working in **front lps** *(see Stitch Guide)* only, ch 1, sc in each st around, join in beg sc, turn.

Rnds 14–21: Working the following rnds in back lps only, ch 3 *(counts as first dc)*, dc in each st around, join in 3rd ch of beg ch-3.

Rnd 22: Ch 2 *(does not count as a st)*, dc in back lp of next st, **fpdc** *(see Stitch Guide)* around next st, [**dc dec** *(see Stitch Guide)* in back lps of next 2 sts, fpdc around next st] around, join in beg dc. *(84 sts)*

Rnds 23 & 24: Ch 3, fpdc around next fpdc, [dc in back lp of next st, fpdc around next fpdc] around, join in 3rd ch of beg ch-3. At end of last rnd, fasten off.

BRIM SIDE
MAKE 2.
Row 1: With size I hook and 1 strand each suede and elastic yarn held tog, ch 28, sc in 2nd ch from hook, sc in each of next 5 chs, [2 sc in next ch, sc in each of next 6 chs] across, turn. *(30 sc)*

Rows 2 & 3: Ch 1, **sc dec** *(see Stitch Guide)* in first 2 sts, sc dec in next 2 sts, sc in each st across to last 4 sts, [sc dec in next 2 sts] twice, turn. *(22 sc at end of last row)*

Row 4: Ch 1, sc dec in first 2 sts, sc in each of next 5 sts, 3 sc in next st, sc in each of next 6 sts, 3 sc in next st, sc in each of next 5 sts, sc dec in last 2 sts, turn. *(24 sc)*

Rows 5 & 6: Rep row 2. *(16 sc at end of last row)*

Row 7: Ch 1, sc dec in first 2 sts, sc in each st across to last 2 sts, sc dec in last 2 sts, turn. *(14 sc)*

Row 8: Rep row 2. Fasten off. *(10 sc)*

Using Brim as a pattern, cut piece from plastic canvas.

With Brim Sides held tog and plastic piece held between, sew Brim Sides tog through back lps.

Sew Brim across last rnd of Hat Front.

Sew 1 side of snap to center of rows 5 and 6 on top side of Brim. Sew other side of snap to rnds 16 and 17 of Hat above first side of snap. ∎

Earflap **Hat**

DESIGN BY ANNA AL

SKILL LEVEL

INTERMEDIATE

FINISHED SIZE

One size fits most adults

MATERIALS

- Bernat Soft Boucle bulky (chunky) weight yarn (5 oz/ 255 yds/140g per ball): 1 ball #6703 natural
- Size I/9/5.5mm crochet hook or size needed to obtain gauge

GAUGE

13 hdc = 4 inches; 14 hdc rows = 4 inches

PATTERN NOTES

Chain-2 at beginning of row or round does not count as first half double crochet unless otherwise stated.

Join with slip stitch as indicated unless otherwise stated.

SPECIAL STITCHES

Front cable: Sk next 4 sts, **fptr** *(see Stitch Guide)* around each of next 4 sts, working in front of last 4 sts worked, fptr around each of 4 sts just sk.

Back cable: Sk next 4 sts, **bptr** *(see Stitch Guide)* around each of next 4 sts, working in back of last 4 sts worked, bptr around each of 4 sts just sk.

INSTRUCTIONS
HAT
BODY

Rnd 1: Ch 3, 8 hdc in 3rd ch from hook *(first 2 chs do not count as first hdc)*, **join** *(see Pattern Notes)* in first hdc. *(8 hdc)*

Rnd 2: Ch 2 *(see Pattern Notes)*, 2 hdc in first st and in each st around, join in beg hdc. *(16 hdc)*

Rnd 3: Ch 2, 2 hdc in first st, hdc in next st, [2 hdc in next st, hdc in next st] around, join in beg hdc. *(24 hdc)*

Rnd 4: Ch 2, 2 hdc in first st, hdc in each of next 2 sts, [2 hdc in next st, hdc in each of next 2 sts] around, join in beg hdc. *(32 hdc)*

Rnd 5: Ch 2, 2 hdc in first st, hdc in each of next 3 sts, [2 hdc in next st, hdc in each of next 3 sts] around, join in beg hdc. *(40 hdc)*

Rnd 6: Ch 2, 2 hdc in first st, hdc in each of next 4 sts, [2 hdc in next st, hdc in each of next 4 sts] around, join in beg hdc. *(48 hdc)*

Rnd 7: Ch 2, 2 hdc in first st, hdc in each of next 4 sts, [**fpdc** *(see Stitch Guide)* around each of next 8 sts, 2 hdc in next st, hdc in next st] 4 times, hdc in each of last 3 sts, join in beg hdc. *(53 sts)*

Rnd 8: Ch 2, 2 hdc in first st, hdc in each of next 5 sts, [**front cable** *(see Special Stitches)* 2 hdc in next st, hdc in each of next 2 sts] 4 times, hdc in each of last 3 sts, join in beg hdc. *(58 sts)*

Rnd 9: Ch 2, 2 hdc in first st, hdc in each of next 6 sts, [fpdc around each of next 8 sts, 2 hdc in next st, hdc in each of next 3 sts] 4 times, hdc in each of last 3 sts, join in beg hdc. *(63 sts)*

Rnds 10 & 11: Ch 2, hdc in each of first 8 sts, [fpdc around each of next 8 sts, hdc in each of next 5 sts] 4 times, hdc in each of last 3 sts, join in beg hdc.

Rnd 12: Ch 2, hdc in each of first 8 sts, [front cable, hdc in each of next 5 sts] 4 times, hdc in each of last 3 sts, join in beg hdc.

Rnds 13 & 14: Rep rnds 10 and 11.

Next rnds: Rep rnds 10–14 once.

Next rnds: Rep rnds 10 and 11 once. At end of last rnd, fasten off.

FIRST EARFLAP

Row 1: Now working in rows, with RS facing, sk first 3 sts, join in next st, ch 2, hdc in same st and in each of next 4 sts, front cable, hdc in each of next 5 sts, leaving rem sts unworked, turn. *(18 sts)*

Row 2: Ch 2, hdc in each of first 5 sts, **bpdc** *(see Stitch Guide)* around each of next 8 sts, hdc in each of last 5 sts, turn.

Row 3: Ch 2, hdc in each of first 5 sts, fpdc around each of next 8 sts, hdc in each of last 5 sts, turn.

Row 4: Rep row 2.

Row 5: Ch 2, **hdc dec** *(see Stitch Guide)* in first 2 sts, hdc in each of next 3 sts, **back cable** *(see Special Stitches)*, hdc in each of next 3 sts, hdc dec in last 2 sts, turn. *(16 sts)*

Row 6: Ch 2, hdc dec in first 2 sts, hdc in each of next 2 sts, fpdc around each of next 8 sts, hdc in each of next 2 sts, hdc dec in last 2 sts, turn. *(14 sts)*

Row 7: Ch 2, hdc dec in first 2 sts, hdc in next st, bpdc around each of next 8 sts, hdc in next st, hdc dec in last 2 sts, turn.

Row 8: Ch 2, hdc dec in first 3sts, fpdc around each of next 6 sts, hdc dec in last 3 sts, turn. *(8 sts)*

Row 9: Ch 2, hdc dec in first 2 sts, hdc in each of next 4 sts, hdc dec in last 2 sts. Fasten off. *(6 sts)*

2ND EARFLAP

Row 1: With RS facing, sk next 21 sts on Body, join in next st, ch 2, hdc in same st and each of next 4 sts, front cable, hdc in each of next 5 sts, leaving rem sts unworked, turn.

Rows 2–9: Rep rows 2–9 of First Earflap.

EDGING

With RS facing, join with sc in center back of Hat, evenly sp sc around, join in beg sc. Fasten off. ■

Felted Floppy Hat

DESIGN BY NAZANIN FARD

SKILL LEVEL

EASY

FINISHED SIZE

22½ inches in circumference, excluding brim

MATERIALS

- Lion Brand Lion Wool medium (worsted) weight yarn (3 oz/ 158 yds/85g per ball): 6 balls #178 dark teal
- Size P/15/10mm crochet hook or size needed to obtain gauge
- Tapestry needle
- Sewing needle
- Matching sewing thread
- 1½ yds ribbon
- 1 flower
- Stitch marker

GAUGE

5 sc = 2 inches

PATTERN NOTE

Join with slip stitch as indicated unless otherwise stated.

INSTRUCTIONS

HAT

Rnd 1: Beg at center of crown, make **slip ring** (*see Fig. 1*), 8 sc in ring, pull short end tight to close center hole. (*8 sc*)

Rnd 2: Ch 1, 2 sc in each sc around, **join** (*see Pattern Note*) in beg sc. (*16 sc*)

Rnd 3: Ch 1, sc in each sc around, join in beg sc.

MEDIUM

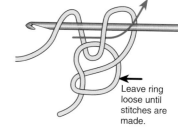

Leave ring loose until stitches are made.

Fig 1.
Slip Ring

Rnd 4: Ch 1, 2 sc in each st around, join in beg sc. (*32 sc*)

Rnd 5: Ch 1, sc in each st around, join in beg sc.

Rnd 6: Ch 1, 2 sc in each st around, join in beg sc. (*64 sc*)

Rnds 7–11: Ch 1, sc in each sc around, join in beg sc.

Rnd 12: Ch 1, sc in first st, 2 sc in next st, [sc in next sc, 2 sc in next sc] around, join in beg sc. (*96 sc*)

Rnd 13–33: Ch 1, sc in each sc around, join in beg sc.

Rnd 34: Ch 1, sc in first st, 2 sc in next st, [sc in next sc, 2 sc in next sc] around, join in beg sc. (*144 sc*)

Rnds 35–44: Ch 1, sc in each sc around, join in beg sc. At end of last rnd, fasten off.

FELTING INSTRUCTIONS

Place Hat in pillowcase. Secure top of pillowcase with rubber band. Fill washing machine with hot water, add some mild detergent. Add pillowcase and a pair of old jeans or towels and let machine run for a few minutes. Remove Hat. Squeeze water out and try Hat on. If Hat fits well, it is time for rinsing. Otherwise rep procedure several times, until Hat is desired size.

For drying Hat, find a bowl about the same size as desired for Hat size. Wrap bowl in clean unmarked plastic bag. Place crown of Hat on bowl and straighten as desired. Let dry.

Trim with ribbon and flower as shown in photo. ■

Post Stitch
BEANIE

DESIGN BY KATHERINE ENG

SKILL LEVEL
■■■□
INTERMEDIATE

FINISHED SIZE
One size fits most adults

MATERIALS

- Lion Brand Jiffy bulky (chunky) weight yarn (2½ oz/117 yds/70g per ball): 1 ball #325 El Paso
- Size K/10½/6.5mm crochet hook or size needed to obtain gauge
- Tapestry needle

GAUGE
Row 1 = 5¼ inches across; rows 1–4 = 2¼ inches

PATTERN NOTE
Join with slip stitch as indicated unless otherwise stated.

INSTRUCTIONS
BEANIE
Row 1: Ch 60, working in **back lps** (*see Stitch Guide*), dc in 6th ch from hook (*first 5 chs count as dc, sk 1 ch and ch-1*), [ch 1, sk next ch, dc in next ch] across, turn. (*29 dc, 28 ch sps*)

Row 2: Ch 1, sc in first st, [ch 1, sk next ch sp, sc in next st] across, turn.

Row 3: Ch 1, sc in first st, [ch 1, sk next ch sp, **fpdc** (*see Stitch Guide*) around st 2 rows below, ch 1, sk next ch sp, sc in next st] across, turn.

Row 4: Ch 1, sc in first st, [ch 1, sk next ch sp, sc in next st] across, turn.

Rows 5–10: [Rep rows 3 and 4 alternately] 3 times.

Row 11: Ch 4 (*counts as first dc and ch-1*), sk next ch sp, dc in next st, [ch 1, sk next ch sp, dc in next st] across, **do not turn**. Leaving long end, fasten off.

TOP
Rnd 1: Now working in rnds, with RS facing, **join** (*see Pattern Note*) in first st of row 11, ch 1, sc in next ch sp and in each ch sp around, join in beg sc. (28 sc)

Rnd 2: Working in back lps, ch 1, sc in each st around, join in beg sc.

Rnd 3: Working back lps, ch 1, sc in first st, ch 1, sk next st, [sc in next st, ch 1, sk next st] around, join in beg sc. (*14 sc*)

Rnd 4: Ch 1, sc in first ch sp, ch 1, sk next st, [sc in next ch sp, ch 1, sk next st] around, join in beg sc.

Rnd 5: Working in back lps, ch 1, sc in each st around, join in beg sc.

Rnd 6: Working in back lps, ch 1, sc in first st, ch 1, sk next st, [sc in next st, ch 1, sk next st] around, join in beg sc. Leaving long end, fasten off.

Weave end through top of sts on rnd 6, pull to close. Secure end.

With long end at end of row 11, sew ends of rows 1–11 tog.

EDGING
Working around starting ch on opposite side of row 1, join with sc in any ch sp, ch 1, [sc in next ch sp, ch 1] around, join in beg sc. ∎

Annie's® *Hooked on Crochet! Hats* is published by Annie's, 306 East Parr Road, Berne, IN 46711. Printed in USA. Copyright © 2008, 2013 Annie's. All rights reserved. This publication may not be reproduced in part or in whole without written permission from the publisher.

RETAIL STORES: If you would like to carry this pattern book or any other Annie's publications, visit AnniesWSL.com.

Every effort has been made to ensure that the instructions in this pattern book are complete and accurate. We cannot, however, take responsibility for human error, typographical mistakes or variations in individual work. Please visit AnniesCustomerCare.com to check for pattern updates.

ISBN: 978-1-59635-229-2
9 10 11 12 13 14

STITCH GUIDE

FOR MORE COMPLETE INFORMATION,
VISIT ANNIESCATALOG.COM/STITCHGUIDE

STITCH ABBREVIATIONS

beg	begin/begins/beginning
bpdc	back post double crochet
bpsc	back post single crochet
bptr	back post treble crochet
CC	contrasting color
ch(s)	chain(s)
ch-	refers to chain or space previously made (i.e., ch-1 space)
ch sp(s)	chain space(s)
cl(s)	cluster(s)
cm	centimeter(s)
dc	double crochet (singular/plural)
dc dec	double crochet 2 or more stitches together, as indicated
dec	decrease/decreases/decreasing
dtr	double treble crochet
ext	extended
fpdc	front post double crochet
fpsc	front post single crochet
fptr	front post treble crochet
g	gram(s)
hdc	half double crochet
hdc dec	half double crochet 2 or more stitches together, as indicated
inc	increase/increases/increasing
lp(s)	loop(s)
MC	main color
mm	millimeter(s)
oz	ounce(s)
pc	popcorn(s)
rem	remain/remains/remaining
rep(s)	repeat(s)
rnd(s)	round(s)
RS	right side
sc	single crochet (singular/plural)
sc dec	single crochet 2 or more stitches together, as indicated
sk	skip/skipped/skipping
sl st(s)	slip stitch(es)
sp(s)	space(s)/spaced
st(s)	stitch(es)
tog	together
tr	treble crochet
trtr	triple treble
WS	wrong side
yd(s)	yard(s)
yo	yarn over

YARN CONVERSION

OUNCES TO GRAMS		GRAMS TO OUNCES	
1	28.4	25	7/8
2	56.7	40	1 2/3
3	85.0	50	1 3/4
4	113.4	100	3 1/2

UNITED STATES		UNITED KINGDOM
sl st (slip stitch)	=	sc (single crochet)
sc (single crochet)	=	dc (double crochet)
hdc (half double crochet)	=	htr (half treble crochet)
dc (double crochet)	=	tr (treble crochet)
tr (treble crochet)	=	dtr (double treble crochet)
dtr (double treble crochet)	=	ttr (triple treble crochet)
skip	=	miss

Single crochet decrease (sc dec): (Insert hook, yo, draw lp through) in each of the sts indicated, yo, draw through all lps on hook.

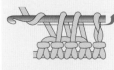

Example of 2-sc dec

Half double crochet decrease (hdc dec): (Yo, insert hook, yo, draw lp through) in each of the sts indicated, yo, draw through all lps on hook.

Example of 2-hdc dec

Reverse single crochet (reverse sc): Ch 1, sk first st, working from left to right, insert hook in next st from front to back, draw up lp on hook, yo and draw through both lps on hook.

Chain (ch): Yo, pull through lp on hook.

Single crochet (sc): Insert hook in st, yo, pull through st, yo, pull through both lps on hook.

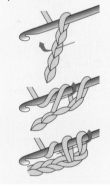

Double crochet (dc): Yo, insert hook in st, yo, pull through st, [yo, pull through 2 lps] twice.

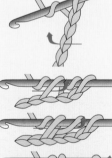
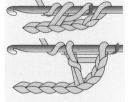

Double crochet decrease (dc dec): (Yo, insert hook, yo, draw lp through, yo, draw through 2 lps on hook) in each of the sts indicated, yo, draw through all lps on hook.

Example of 2-dc dec

Front loop (front lp) Back loop (back lp)

Front Loop   Back Loop

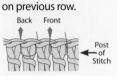

Front post stitch (fp): Back post stitch (bp): When working post st, insert hook from right to left around post of st on previous row.

Back   Front

Post of Stitch

Half double crochet (hdc): Yo, insert hook in st, yo, pull through st, yo, pull through all 3 lps on hook.

Double treble crochet (dtr): Yo 3 times, insert hook in st, yo, pull through st, [yo, pull through 2 lps] 4 times.

Treble crochet decrease (tr dec): Holding back last lp of each st, tr in each of the sts indicated, yo, pull through all lps on hook.

Example of 2-tr dec

Slip stitch (sl st): Insert hook in st, pull through both lps on hook.

Chain color change (ch color change) Yo with new color, draw through last lp on hook.

Double crochet color change (dc color change) Drop first color, yo with new color, draw through last 2 lps of st.

Treble crochet (tr): Yo twice, insert hook in st, yo, pull through st, [yo, pull through 2 lps] 3 times.

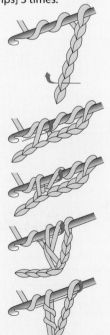